# The Other Voice

# The Other Voice

Translations from the *Übertragungen* of Paul Celan

Holly Cundiff

Marquand Books
*Seattle*

# Contents

# Preface

*Thinking and thanking in our language are words from one and the same source. Whoever follows out their meaning enters the semantic field of: "recollect," "bear in mind," "remembrance," "devotion." Permit me, from this standpoint, to thank you.*

—Paul Celan, Bremen Prize acceptance speech, 1958

These eighteen translations by Paul Celan were written or later revised between 1947 and 1968, when he worked on the vast bulk of his interpretations. He transformed the poems of Emily Dickinson, William Shakespeare, Giuseppe Ungaretti, and others (in all, forty-five authors from seven languages) into German, the language of his beloved mother, who died in a concentration camp in 1942, and the language of his tormentors, the German Reich. Celan was released from a labor camp in 1944 yet never spoke about his experiences, channeling them instead into his own poetry and masterfully instilling a sense of foreboding and danger into many of the translations found here. Celan wrote of poetry, "And are these paths only detours, detours from you to you? But they are, among how many others, the paths on which language becomes voice. They are encounters, paths from a voice to a listening you, natural paths."* In presenting this multivariant language cycle, it is my hope that Paul Celan would approve.

—Holly Cundiff

* From his speech "Meridian," cited in *Corona: Selected Poems of Paul Celan*, trans. Susan H. Gillespie (Barrytown, NY: Station Hill of Barrytown, 2013), xx.

*for Michael Brophy*

# The Other Voice

1. Giuseppe Ungaretti

# Canto a due voci

PRIMA VOCE

Il cuore mi è crudele:

Ama né altrove troveresti fuoco

Nel rinnovargli strazi tanto vigile:

Lontano dal tuo amore

Soffocato da tenebra si avventa

E quando, per guardare nel suo baratro,

Arretri smemorandoti

In te gli occhi e l'agguanti,

Lo fulmina la brama,

L'unica luce sua che dal segreto

Suo incendio può guizzare.

*Roma, Domenica–Giovedí 10–14 Maggio 1959*

ALTRA VOCE

*Piú nulla gli si può nel cuore smuovere,*

*Piú nel suo cuore nulla*

*Se non acri sorprese del ricordo*

*In una carne logora?*

PAUL CELAN (TRANS.)

# Gesang, Zweistimmig

DIE ERSTE STIMME

Das Herz ist grausam zu mir:

Es liebt, und auch sonstwo fändst du kein Feuer,

wachsam wie dies beim Erneuern der Pein:

Weitab von deiner Liebe,

gewürgt von Finsternis, stürzt es los,

und wenn du, zu schaun seinen Abgrund,

die Augen zurücknimmst in dich,

gedächtnislos, und es packst,

blitzt das Verlangen es nieder,

das einzige Licht, das aufzucken kann

aus seinem geheimen Brand.

*Rom, Sonntag–Donnerstag 10.–14. Mai 1959*

## DIE ANDERE STIMME

*Ihm kannst du nichts mehr bewegen im Herzen*

*nichts mehr in seinem Herzen,*

*es sei denn herbes Herauf des Erinnerns*

*in einem aufgeriebenen Fleisch.*

Holly Cundiff (trans.)

# Song, in Two Voices

THE FIRST VOICE

The cruel heart:

It loves, without fire.

Aware how this suffering renews,

Far away from your love.

Retching from evil, it tumbles away,

And if you look for its pit,

With that gaze recoiling within you,

Forgetting, and seizing it,

That explosive passion,

The only light, able to catch fire

Out of its secret flame.

*Rome, Sunday–Thursday 10–14 May 1959*

## THE OTHER VOICE

*You can no longer stir his heart*

*nothing more to move in his heart*

*for it would be a bitter upstream of remembrance*

*in tormented flesh.*

2. GIUSEPPE UNGARETTI

# Variazioni su nulla

Quel nonnulla di sabbia che trascorre
Dalla clessidra muto e va posandosi,
E, fugaci, le impronte sul carnato,
Sul carnato che muore, d'una nube . . .

Poi mano che rovescia la clessidra,
Il ritorno per muoversi, di sabbia,
Il farsi argentea tacito di nube
Ai primi brevi lividi dell'alba . . .

La mano in ombra la clessidra volse,
E, di sabbia, il nonnulla che trascorre
Silente, è unica cosa che ormai s'oda
E, essendo udita, in buio non scompaia.

Paul Celan (trans.)

# Variationen über Nichts

Dies Nichts an Sand, das die stumme
Sanduhr durchrinnt und hingeht und sich setzt,
und jene Spuren, flüchtig, auf dem Inkarnat,
die Spuren einer Wolke auf dem Inkarnat, das hinstirbt . . .

Dann eine Hand, die kehrt die Sanduhr um,
des Sandes Rückkehr zur Bewegung,
das Sich-zu-Silber-Fügen, stumm, der einen Wolke
beim ersten fahlen Aufzucken des Tags . . .

Die Hand im Schatten kippt' die Sanduhr um,
und jenes Nichts an Sand, das still
hindurchrinnt, es ist alles, was man fortan hört,
und, da's gehört wird, geht es nicht ins Dunkel ein.

Holly Cundiff (trans.)

# Variations across Nothingness

This nothingness in sand, that sand in the mute
hourglass wending and slipping and sinking,
and those traces, hurrying towards it incarnadine,
the traces cloudy towards it incarnadine, this passing . . .

Then a hand, which turns the hourglass over,
in which sand returns home with motion,
that yourselves-with-silver-join'd, mute with the gather'd clouds
with the first pale lighting the following day . . .

The hand in the shadows turns the hourglass over,
and that nothingness in sand, silent
throughout, is all that anyone afterward has ever heard,
and it was heard, never departing with the darkness.

3. Arthur Rimbaud

# Bateau ivre

Comme je descendais des Fleuves impassibles,
Je ne me sentis plus guidé par les haleurs:
Des Peaux-rouges criards les avaient pris pour cibles,
Les ayant cloués nus aux poteaux de couleurs.

J'étais insoucieux de tous les équipages,
Porteur de blés flamands ou de cotons anglais.
Quand avec mes haleurs ont fini ces tapages
Les Fleuves m'ont laissé descendre où je voulais.

Dans les clapotements furieux des marées
Moi, l'autre hiver, plus sourd que les cerveaux d'enfants,
Je courus! Et les Péninsules démarrées
N'ont pas subi tohu-bohus plus triomphants.

La tempête a béni mes éveils maritimes.
Plus léger qu'un bouchon j'ai dansé sur les flots
Qu'on appelle rouleurs éternels de victimes,
Dix nuits, sans regretter l'oeil niais des falots!

Plus douce qu'aux enfants la chair des pommes sures,
L'eau verte pénétra ma coque de sapin
Et des taches de vins bleus et des vomissures
Me lava, dispersant gouvernail et grappin.

Et dès lors, je me suis baigné dans le Poème
De la Mer, infusé d'astres, et lactescent,
Dévorant les azurs verts; où, flottaison blême
Et ravie, un noyé pensif parfois descend;

Où, teignant tout à coup les bleuités, délires
Et rythmes lents sous les rutilements du jour,
Plus fortes que l'alcool, plus vastes que nos lyres,
Fermentent les rousseurs amères de l'amour!

Je sais les cieux crevant en éclairs, et les trombes
Et les ressacs et les courants: Je sais le soir,
L'Aube exaltée ainsi qu'un peuple de colombes,
Et j'ai vu quelquefois ce que l'homme a cru voir!

J'ai vu le soleil bas, taché d'horreurs mystiques,
Illuminant de longs figements violets,
Pareils à des acteurs de drames très antiques
Les flots roulant au loin leurs frissons de volets!

J'ai rêvé la nuit verte aux neiges éblouies,
Baiser montant aux yeux des mers avec lenteur,
La circulation des sèves inouïes,
Et l'éveil jaune et bleu des phosphores chanteurs!

J'ai suivi, des mois pleins, pareille aux vacheries
Hystériques, la houle à l'assaut des récifs,
Sans songer que les pieds lumineux des Maries
Pussent forcer le mufle aux Océans poussifs!

J'ai heurté, savez-vous, d'incroyables Florides
Mêlant aux fleurs des yeux de panthères à peaux
D'hommes! Des arcs-en-ciel tendus comme des brides
Sous l'horizon des mers, à de glauques troupeaux!

J'ai vu fermenter les marais énormes, nasses
Où pourrit dans les joncs tout un Léviathan!
Des écroulements d'eaux au milieu des bonaces,
Et les lointains vers les gouffres cataractant!

Glaciers, soleils d'argent, flots nacreux, cieux de braises,
Échouages hideux au fond des golfes bruns
Où les serpents géants dévorés des punaises
Choient, des arbres tordus, avec de noirs parfums!

J'aurais voulu montrer aux enfants ces dorades
Du flot bleu, ces poissons d'or, ces poissons chantants.
– Des écumes de fleurs ont bercé mes dérades
Et d'ineffables vents m'ont ailé par instants.

Parfois martyr lassé des pôles et des zones,
La mer dont le sanglot faisait mon roulis doux
Montait vers moi ses fleurs d'ombre aux ventouses jaunes
Et je restais, ainsi qu'une femme à genoux . . .

Presque île, ballottant sur mes bords les querelles
Et les fientes d'oiseaux clabaudeurs aux yeux blonds.
Et je voguais, lorsqu'à travers mes liens frêles
Des noyés descendaient dormir, à reculons! . . .

Or moi, bateau perdu sous les cheveux des anses,
Jeté par l'ouragan dans l'éther sans oiseau,
Moi dont les Monitors et les voiliers des Hanses
N'auraient pas repêché la carcasse ivre d'eau;

Libre, fumant, monté de brumes violettes,
Moi qui trouais le ciel rougeoyant comme un mur
Qui porte, confiture exquise aux bons poètes,
Des lichens de soleil et des morves d'azur;

Qui courais, taché de lunules électriques,
Planche folle, escorté des hippocampes noirs,
Quand les juillets faisaient crouler à coups de triques
Les cieux ultramarins aux ardents entonnoirs;

Moi qui tremblais, sentant geindre à cinquante lieues
Le rut des Béhémots et les Maelstroms épais,
Fileur éternel des immobilités bleues,
Je regrette l'Europe aux anciens parapets!

J'ai vu des archipels sidéraux! et des îles
Dont les cieux délirants sont ouverts au vogueur:
– Est-ce en ces nuits sans fond que tu dors et t'exiles,
Million d'oiseaux d'or, ô future Vigueur? –

Mais, vrai, j'ai trop pleuré! Les Aubes sont navrantes.
Toute lune est atroce et tout soleil amer:
L'âcre amour m'a gonflé de torpeurs enivrantes.
Ô que ma quille éclate! Ô que j'aille à la mer!

Si je désire une eau d'Europe, c'est la flache
Noire et froide où vers le crépuscule embaumé
Un enfant accroupi plein de tristesses, lâche
Un bateau frêle comme un papillon de mai.

Je ne puis plus, baigné de vos langueurs, ô lames,
Enlever leur sillage aux porteurs de cotons,
Ni traverser l'orgueil des drapeaux et des flammes,
Ni nager sous les yeux horribles des pontons!

Paul Celan (trans.)

# Das trunkene Schiff

Hinab glitt ich die Flüsse, von träger Flut getragen,
da fühlte ich: es zogen die Treidler mich nicht mehr.
Sie waren, von Indianern ans Marterholz geschlagen,
ein Ziel an buntem Pfahle, Gejohle um sich her.

Ich scherte mich den Teufel um Männer und um Frachten;
wars flämisch Korn, wars Wolle, mir war es einerlei.
Vorbei war der Spektakel, den sie am Ufer machten,
hinunter gings die Flüsse, wohin, das stand mir frei.

Derweil die Tide tobte und klatschte an den Dämmen,
flog ich, und es war Winter, wie Kinderhirne stumpf,
dahin. Und wär es möglich, daß jemals Inseln schwämmen,
kein solcher Gischt umbraust' sie, kein ähnlicher Triumph.

Ein leichter Korken, tanzt ich dahin auf steiler Welle:
die erste Meerfahrt haben die Stürme benedeit.
Von solcher Welle heißt es, sie töte und sie fälle –
Die albernen Laternen der Häfen blieben weit!

So süß kann Kindermündern kein grüner Apfel schmecken,
wie mir das Wasser schmeckte, das grün durchs Holz mir drang.
Rein wuschs mich vom Gespeie und von den Blauweinflecken,
fort schleudert es das Steuer, der Draggen barst und sank.

Des Meers Gedicht! Jetzt konnt ich mich frei darin ergehen,
Grünhimmel trank ich, Sterne, taucht ein in milchigen Strahl
und konnt die Wasserleichen zur Tiefe gehen sehen:
ein Treibgut, das versonnen und selig war und fahl.

Die Rhythmen und Delirien, das Blau im rauchigen Schleier,
verfärbt sind sie im Nu hier, versengt sind sie, verzehrt:
so brannnte noch kein Branntwein, kein Lied und keine Leier,
wie hier das bittre Rostrot der Liebe brennt und gärt!

Ich weiß, wie Himmel bersten, ich kenn die Dämmerungen,
die Strömung und die Dünung, die Woge, die sich bäumt,
die Früh – verzückt wie Tauben, die sich emporgeschwungen,
und manchmal sah mein Auge, was Menschenauge träumt.

Ich sah die Sonne hängen – mystisch geflecktes Grauen,
und violett, geronnen, Leuchtstreifen, endlos weit,
und sah die Fluten schaufeln und groß die Bühne bauen,
ein Schauspiel sah ich spielen, das alt war wie die Zeit!

Im Traum sah ich die Schneenacht, die grüne, sich erheben:
ein Kuß stieg zu den Augen der Meeres-Au empor.
Ein Kreisen wars von Säften, ein unerhörtes Weben,
und blau und gelb erwachte der singende Phosphor!

Ich folgt und folgt der Horde von wildgewordnen Kühen:
der See, die Klippen stürmte, folgt ich auf ihrem Ritt.
Vergessen wart ihr, Füße der leuchtenden Marien:
hier keuchten Meeresmäuler – sie schloß kein Heiligentritt!

Wißt ihr, ich lief auf Land auf, wie ihrs nicht schaut im Traume:
Des Menschenpanthers Augen – den Blumen beigesellt!
Ich sah im weitgespannten, im Regenbogenzaume
flutgrün die Herden ziehen am Grund der Meereswelt.

Ich sah, wie's in den Sümpfen, den Riesenreusen, gärte,
darin den Leviathan, verwesend zwischen Tang.
Und Wasserstürze sah ich, wo sich die Stille mehrte,
und schaute, wie die Ferne zur Tiefe niedersank!

Sah Gletscher, Silbersonnen, Gluthimmel, Perlmuttfluten,
den braunen Golf, wo greulich ein Wrack beim andern steht,
und sah die Riesenschlange, ein Fraß der Wanzenbruten,
vom Krüppelbaume fallen, von schwarzem Duft umweht!

Wo seid ihr, Kinderaugen, zu schaun die Herrlichkeiten?
Das Schuppengold der Welle, den Goldfisch, der da singt!
– Dies schaumumblühte Driften, dies Zwischen-Blumen-Gleiten!
Der Wind, der Wind unsäglich, der meine Fahrt beschwingt!

Und litt ich Pein, der Pole und Wendekreise müde,
so schluchzt' es in den Wassern, ich schlingerte dahin,
mit gelbem Saugnapf tauchte empor die Schattenblüte –
ein Weib, so blieb ich liegen, ein Weib auf Weibesknien.

Gewölle und Gezänke hab ich an Bord genommen,
ich war das Vogel-Eiland – blond äugte, was da flog.
Ich trieb mit loser Spante, ich schwamm und ward durchschwommen:
ein Leichnam um den andern, der rücklings schlafwärts zog.

Und ich – verstrickt, verloren im Haar geheimer Buchten,
hinauf ins Vogellose geworfen vom Orkan:
sie fahren nicht, die Klipper, die Koggen, die mich suchten,
des wassertrunknen Rumpfes nimmt sich kein Schlepptau an.

Frei war ich und ich rauchte, von Nebelblau bestiegen,
ich stieß durch Feuerhimmel, ich stieß sie alle ein,
und was den Dichtern mundet, das fühlt ich auf mir liegen:
es waren Sonnenflechten, es war azurner Schleim.

Ich – mondgefleckt, elektrisch: die tollgewordne Planke!
Seepferdchen kam in Scharen und war mein schwarzer Troß.
Ihr Himmel blau und tiefblau, ich sah euch alle wanken,
ich sah, wie euch der Juli durch Glutentrichter goß!

Der Behemoth, der Mahlstrom durchstöhnte jene Breiten,
ich spürte beider Brunstlaut – ein Schauder ging durch mich,
ich schwamm und schwamm durch blaue, durch Regungslosigkeiten –
Europa, deine Wehren, die alten misse ich!

Und ich sah Inselsterne, sah Archipele ragen,
darüber Fieberhimmel – das Tor der Wanderschaft!
– Hats dich dorthin, ins Nächtige und Nächtigste verschlagen,
du goldnes Vogeltausend, du künftige, du Kraft?

Doch wahr, genug des Weinens! Der Morgen muß enttäuschen.
Ob Nacht-, ob Taggestirne, keins, das nicht bitter wär;
ich schwoll von herber Liebe, erstarrt in Liebesräuschen –
O du mein Kiel, zersplittre! Und über mir sei, Meer!

Und gäb es in Europa ein Wasser, das mich lockte,
so wärs ein schwarzer Tümpel, kalt, in der Dämmernis,
an dem dann eins der Kinder, voll Traurigkeiten, hockte
und Boote, falterschwache, und Schiffschen segeln ließ.

Wen du umschmiegt hast, Woge, um den ist es geschehen,
der zieht nicht hinter Frachtern und Baumwollträgern her!
Nie komm ich da vorüber, wo sich die Fahnen blähen,
und wo die Brücken glotzen, da schwimm ich nimmermehr!

Holly Cundiff (trans.)

# The Drunken Ship

I was borne down the river, from weary tide,
Sensing: they're pulling these tow ropes no more.
They were beaten there by Indians at the stake,
A target on colorful totem poles, whooping all around.

The devil if I cared for my men or cargo;
Was it Flemish grain or wool, to me it was the same.
Gone was the fracas they made on the shore,
I existed freely, the rivers coursing smoothly.

While the tide raged and crashed on the dikes,
and it was winter, dull as brains of children, me flying
then. And were it possible that islands ever floated
no spume roared around them like this, nothing triumphant.

One corked, lighter, dancing there on a surging wave:
the first sea voyage held this blessed tempest
of such waves as this it's said that they destroyed and they fell'd –
The ludicrous lanterns from the harbor away!

No child's mouth knows green apples tasting so sweet,
how to me the waters tasted, the green bursting through the wood.
It washed me clean, from the vomit and the blue flecked stains,
catapulted from the rudder, the anchor cracked and sank.

The sea's poem! Now I could freely wander there,
drinking green heaven I, a bright star, plunged into a lacteous light beam
and could see in the water corpses drift towards the depths:
On flotsam, dreamy, blessed and pale.

These rhythms of delirium, smoking in the blue veil,
stained in the twinkling of an eye here, they were singed, consumed:
no brandy did burn, no song nor melody,
as the bitter rust red of love did burn and ferment here!

I know how skies burst, I know the dawns,
the teeming and the swelling, the billows themselves writhing,
the dove-enraptured dawn that itself soared,
And my eyes sometimes seeing what other eyes had dreamed.

I saw the mysterious sun's mottled dawn hanging,
and violet, congealing, streaks twinkling endlessly far,
and saw the flood scooping and the vast theatre created,
I saw a spectacle performed as old as time!

In a dream I saw the snowy night, green, arising:
A kiss swelling the sea-meadow's eyelids on high
an unheard of web, of juices spinning
And yellow-blue awakened the singing phosphorous!

I watched and followed the herd of cows become wild:
The reefs raging at sea I trailed for their ride.
Forgotten you were, feet of the luminous Marias:
Here cower the sea's jaws – closed they're no sanctuary!

You know, I criss-crossed toward the land as I'd seen in a dream
of the eyes of human panthers mingling with flowers!
I saw in the wide-ranging, in the reins of the rainbow,
moving all around the ocean floor, the green herd surging.

I saw, saw in the quagmire, an ogress floating, fermenting,
in which the Leviathan was putrefying amongst the seaweed.
Where their silence grew I saw waterfalls
and watched how the depths in the distance sank!

Seeing glaciers, silvery-suns, burning-heavens, flowing mother of pearl,
the brown gulf, where one frightful wreck stood close to the next,
and seeing the giant boa, a feast for bugs, then
fall from a crippled tree, from a black noxious haze.

Eyes of children, where are you to behold the magnificence?
The wending gold of the wave, the goldfish, here they sing!
The blossoming foam drifting, gliding among the flowers!
The wind, the wind untold, intoning the cheerful voyage!

The turning circle and weary pole, I sang suffering,
I wended there, gulping sobs in the waters this way,
lifting shadowy blossoms aloft with yellowing suction cups –
I thus remained crouching, a woman on her knees, a woman.

Amid squabbling and bickering I was seized aboard,
flying there, I was a pale-eyed bird-land.
I drifted by loosely drawn, I swam and was swum through:
A corpse among the others, drawn backwards into sleep.

Lost in the hair of the sacred bay entangled
upward in derelict flight with the hurricane:
The ship hunting for me, the klipper, hadn't left
The waterlogged carcass itself grasping at no tow rope.

I was smoking and free, ascending out of a blue haze,
I smashed through burning skies, exhausted I smashed through them all,
I sensed lying by me, what the poets had relished:
It was woven sunlight, it was slimy blue sky.

Myself – electric, dappled moonlight: a wild deck!
Seahorses had appeared in dark swarms, my following
I saw you exhausted staggering, your heavens ocean-blue
I saw how throughout July you reigned, incandescent decisive blows.

The maelstrom groaning those distances, the behemoth,
A shudder running through me – I sensed the two loudly rutting.
Completely motionless, I sponged and sponged through blueness –
your ancient resistance, Europe, that I miss!

And I saw the starry lands, saw archipelagos rising
the gateway to the journey meanwhile – feverish skies!
Possessing thee out there, most nocturnal nightfall,
your strength, your future, your thousand golden birds?

True, enough of tears! The morning bound to disillusion
whether night – whether starry dawn, neither bitter.
I swelled from acrid love, paralyzed in lovesickness –
O Sea, reign above me! Split, my keel!

And were there bodies of water in Europe to lure me,
thus it was a blackened murky pool, cold at daybreak,
full of mourning, one child was squatting,
and boats, fragile moths, were sailing well.

Round whom your caresses swirl, waves, t'is that one's lot
Who does not tug behind cargo nor cotton to fabric here!
Never shall I cross where flags are waving,
and where bridges gape open, I swim nevermore!

4. William Shakespeare

# Sonnet I

From fairest creatures we desire increase,
That thereby beauty's rose might never die,
But as the riper should by time decease,
His tender heir might bear his memory:

But thou, contracted to thine own bright eyes,
Feed'st thy light's flame with self-substantial fuel,
Making a famine where abundance lies,
Thyself thy foe, to thy sweet self too cruel.

Thou that art now the world's fresh ornament
And only herald to the gaudy spring,
Within thine own bud buriest thy content,
And, tender churl, mak'st waste in niggarding:

Pity the world, or else this glutton be –
To eat the world's due, by the grave and thee.

Paul Celan (trans.)

# Sonett I

Was west und schön ist, du erhoffst ein Mehr
von ihm: die Rose Schönheit soll nicht sterben.
Und gibt sie, die gezeitigte, die Krone her,
so wahre, was sie war, ihr zarter Erbe.

Doch du, ins eigne Auge eingeengt,
verbrauchst dich selbst, daß deine Flamme loht,
du darbst und hungerst, überreich beschenkt,
und bist, der dich am grausamsten bedroht.

Kein Schmuck wie du, den sich ein Jahr je gab;
kein solcher Herold seiner Farbenfreuden;
doch du: die eigne Knospe ist dein Grab,
ein einzig Knausern bist du im Vergeuden.

Denk an die Welt und was ihr Erbteil ist,
du, der du dich nicht sattgräbst und es frißt.

Holly Cundiff (trans.)

# Sonnet I

What fair creature, thou desire only more
Of him: that beautiful rose shall not die,
Should it surrender, this place, that crown,
Like this there's, whatever thou be, her delicate legacy.

Nevertheless you, in your own eye penitent
Consuming yourself in your blazing flame,
You desire and hunger, lavish gifts,
And her, who you cruelest threaten.

None decorous such as you, yourself one year always gives
No one thus herald he more colorfully;
Nevertheless you: that tender-bud unconventionality is your grave.
One only miserly he you squander within.

Ponder on that world and what her inheritance is,
You, who you yourself won't dig a grave that they devour.

5. William Shakespeare

# Sonnet II

When forty winters shall besiege thy brow,
And dig deep trenches in thy beauty's field,
Thy youth's proud livery, so gaz'd on now,
Will be a totter'd weed of small worth held:

Then being ask'd where all thy beauty lies,
Where all the treasure of thy lusty days,
To say within thine own deep sunken eyes
Were an all-eating shame, and thriftless praise.

How much more praise deserv'd thy beauty's use
If thou couldst answer: "This fair child of mine
Shall sum my count, and make my old excuse", –
Proving his beauty by succession thine!

This were to be new made when thou art old,
And see thy blood warm when thou feel'st it cold.

Paul Celan (trans.)

# Sonett II

Wenn vierzig Winter deine Stirn umdrängen,
der Schönheit Flur voll Furchen steht, verheert,
und deiner Jugend Kleid, dran soviel Augen hängen,
ist Plunder, Kram, und keinen Groschen wert,

wirst, da sie dich nach ihr, der Schönheit, fragen,
nach all der Tage und der Schätze Ort,
du dies: <<Beim eingesunknen Auge>> sagen?
So spräche Scham, ein Unwort wär dies Wort.

Ein Wort sprächst du, der Schönheit angemessen,
indem du sprächst: <<Mein ists, dies schöne Kind.
Es setzt mich fort, ich bin, bin unvergessen.>>
Seht, wie die Schönheit mit ihm neu beginnt.

So wärst du, altgeworden, nimmer alt.
Wer sagt, dein Blut verebbe? Nein, es wallt.

HOLLY CUNDIFF (TRANS.)

# Sonnet II

Even though forty winters furrow your brow
this beautiful wrinkle-filled field, devastated,
and you of garbed youth, disoriented however much see hanging,
your plundering, pilfering, worth no penny,

thence, in it yourself for her, ask this beauty
for all the days and the love here,
you then: "with sunken eyes" say?
Speak shamelessly like this, one meaningless it's this word

you would speak one word, this beauty fair.
As you would say: "My one, beautiful child,
it moved me away, that's me, me unforgotten."
Sees, how its beauty with him began anew.

The way was you, aging, never aged.
Who says, your blood subsides? No, it surges.

6. William Shakespeare

# Sonnet LVII

Being your slave, what should I do but tend
Upon the hours and times of your desire?
I have no precious time at all to spend,
Nor services to do, till you require.

Nor dare I chide the world-without-end hour
Whilst I, my sovereign, watch the clock for you.
Nor think the bitterness of absence sour
When you have bid your servant once adieu;

Nor dare I question with my jealous thought
Where you may be, or your affairs suppose,
But like a sad slave stay and think of nought
Save where you are how happy you make those.

So true a fool is love that in your will,
Though you do anything, he thinks no ill.

Paul Celan (trans.)

# Sonett LVII

Da ich dein Sklave bin, was kann ich tun, als deinen
Wünschen entgegenharrn die Stunden lang, die Tage?
Die Zeit, die kostbarste, ist mir wie irgendeine.
Und Dienste? Keinerlei, eh du's mir aufgetragen.

Die Fristen, weltenlang, ich wag sie nicht zu schelten,
wenn ich, mein Herr und Fürst, verfolg der Zeiger Kreisen.
Abwesenheit – sie kann mir nimmer bitter gelten,
wenn du das Abschiedswort gesprochen vor der Reise.

Kein Fragen kommt mich an, kein eifersüchtig Denken
an deinen Aufenthalt, das Fernsein, die Geschäfte.
Doch muß an jene dort, an die von dir Beschenkten,
dein trauriger, dein Knecht die leeren Blicke heften.

Solch treuer Narr ist Liebe: nimmer sieht
sie Arg in deinem Tun – was auch geschieht.

Holly Cundiff (trans.)

# Sonnet LVII

Since I'm your slave, what can I do, but
wait wanting against those long hours, those days?
This time, this preciousness, is to me as any other.
And duties? Till you have entrusted them to me I have none.

I never dare scold at the world-without-end hour
as I, my sovereign and master, fixate on time.
Absence – I can never regard it as something bitter,
when you have spoken words of farewell before the voyage.

No questions come to me, no jealous thoughts
your layover far away, those affairs.
Yet, on those to whom you benefit, your slave
your sad one, must raise his empty glances.

Such a trusting fool is love: he never sees
guile in what you do – whatever happens.

7. William Shakespeare

# Sonnet LXXI

No longer mourn for me when I am dead
Than you shall hear the surly sullen bell
Give warning to the world that I am fled
From this vile world with vilest worms to dwell:

Nay, if you read this line, remember not
The hand that writ it, for I love you so
That I in your sweet thoughts would be forgot
If thinking on me then should make you woe.

Oh if, I say, you look upon this verse
When I perhaps compounded am with clay,
Do not so much as my poor name rehearse,
But let your love even with my life decay;

Lest the wise world should look into your moan,
And mock you with me after I am gone.

Paul Celan (trans.)

# Sonett LXXI

Du sollst, bin ich hinweg, so lang nur klagen,
als du die Glocke hörst, die düstere, vom Turm;
so lange, als die bracht, der Welt zu sagen:
Der bei dir wohnte, ging und wohnt beim Wurm.

Dies schreibe ich, doch du, hast du's gelesen,
vergiß, wers schrieb. Denn sieh, ich liebe dich:
ich wollt, ich wäre nie in deinem Sinn gewesen,
wenn, da du mein gedenkst, dich Gram beschlich'.

Du laß, ruht einst dein Blick auf diesen Worten,
derweil ich Staub bin, Staub bin und nicht mehr,
die Liebe werden, was auch ich geworden,
und meinen Namen, sag ihn nicht mehr her:

Die Welt, klugäugig, sucht schon deine Tränen,
mich, da ich fort bin, mit dir zu verhöhnen.

Holly Cundiff (trans.)

# Sonnet LXXI

You should lament when I am dead, as long as
you hear the somber-bell in the tower;
say to the world, as long as it needs:
the one who dwelled with you, left and dwells with the worms.

This I write, yet if you have read it,
forget who wrote it. As I love you:
I love you, wish I'd never even been sensed by you,
If thoughts of me bring you sadness.

If your glance should ever alight upon these words,
while I am dust, am dust and no more,
let this love become what I've become as well,
and my name I shall no longer recite.

The wise-eyed world seeks your tears
to mock you with me here, since I am gone.

8. William Shakespeare

# Sonnet CVII

Not mine own fears, nor the prophetic soul
Of the wide world dreaming on things to come,
Can yet the lease of my true love control,
Suppos'd as forfeit to a confin'd doom.

The mortal moon hath her eclipse endur'd,
And the sad augurs mock their own presage;
Incertainties now crown themselves assur'd,
And peace proclaims olives of endless age.

Now with the drops of this most balmy time
My love looks fresh; and Death to me subscribes,
Since spite of him I'll live in this poor rhyme
While he insults o'er dull and speechless tribes:

And thou in this shalt find thy monument
When tyrants' crests and tombs of brass are spent.

Paul Celan (trans.)

# Sonett CVII

Nicht Angst, mir eigen, nicht der weltenweiten
Wahrträume Sinn für Dinge, die da kommen, kann
bemessen meiner Liebe Fristen oder Zeiten,
entgrenzt und unverwirkt ist sie, in niemands Bann.

Der Mond, der sterbliche, verschattete: er blinkt!
Augurenwort, dir war Augurenspott beschieden.
Das Schwankende von einst? Gekrönt und unbedingt.
Und mit dem alterslosen Ölzweig kommt der Frieden.

Umbalsamt, meine Liebe, bist du, bist umtaut
von frischer Zeit – kein Tod, dich fortzuschwemmen.
Ich lebe, ihm zum Trotz, im Reim, den ich gebaut,
derweil er dumpfen grollt und sprachenlosen Stämmen.

Und du: in diesem hier, da steht es noch, dein Bild,
wenn Gräbererz verwittert und Tyrannenschild.

Holly Cundiff (trans.)

# Sonnet CVII

Not my own fears, nor the world-wide
dreams of things to come, can
figure the bounds of my love or waiting,
it is unbounded and everlasting under no one's spell.

The mortal moon, once obscured, is gleaming through!
It was your lot that augurs' words be made into mockery.
The uncertainties from long ago? Crowned and absolute.
And timeless my olive branch comes in peace.

Balsamy my love, you are bathed, bathed in dew,
fresh of time, not death to cleanse you from.
I live for the spite in the rhyme that I've built,
The while he growls at tribes dim and tongue-tied.

And here, in this place, here your image still,
When graves of brass have weather'd and tyrants' shields decay'd.

9. Stéphane Mallarmé

# Rondel

Si tu veux nous nous aimerons
Avec tes lèvres sans le dire
Cette rose ne l'interromps
Qu'à verser un silence pire

Jamais de chants ne lancent prompts
Le scintillement du sourire
Si tu veux nous nous aimerons
Avec tes lèvres sans le dire

Muet muet entre les ronds
Sylphe dans la pourpre d'empire
Un baiser flambant se déchire
Jusqu'aux pointes des ailerons
Si tu veux nous nous aimerons.

Paul Celan (trans.)

# Rondel

Willst du's, solls die Liebe sein,
Du, dein Mund, wir sagens nicht,
Schenkst der Rose Schweigen ein,
Bittrer, so du's unterbrichst.

Lieder, willig, schicken kein
Lächeln, sprühen uns kein Licht,
Willst du's, solls die Liebe sein,
Du, dein Mund, wir sagens nicht.

Stumm-und-stumm, hier zwischenein,
Sylphe, purpurn, kaiserlich,
Flammt ein Kuß, schon teilt er sich,
Flügelspitzen flackern, fein,
Willst du's, solls die Liebe sein.

Holly Cundiff (trans.)

# Circle

If you want it, it must be love,
You, your mouth, we never say it,
pouring the silence of the rose,
wicked tongued, you interrupt it.

No smiles willingly sent us songs,
nor shower sparkly light,
if you want it, it must be love,
you, your mouth, we never say it.

Dumb and secret, here between,
imperial crimson sylph,
parted, if a kiss takes flame,
delicate flickering wing-tip,
if you want it, it must be love.

10. Osip Mandelstam

# Концерт на вокзале

Нельзя дышать, и твердь кишит червями,
И ни одна звезда не говорит,
Но, видит Бог, есть музыка над нами,
Дрожит вокзал от пенья аонид
И снова, паровозными свистками
Разорванный, скрипичный воздух слит.

Огромный парк. Вокзала шар стеклянный.
Железный мир опять заворожен.
На звучный пир в элизиум туманный
Торжественно уносится вагон.
Павлиний крик и рокот фортепьянный -
Я опоздал. Мне страшно. Это сон.

И я вхожу в стеклянный лес вокзала,
Скрипичный строй в смятеньи и в слезах.
Ночного хора дикое начало,
И запах роз в гниющих парниках,
Где под стеклянным небом ночевала
Родная тень в кочующих толпах.

И мнится мне: весь в музыке и пене
Железный мир так нищенски дрожит,
В стеклянные я упираюсь сени;
Куда же ты? На тризне милой тени
В последний раз нам музыка звучит.

1921

PAUL CELAN (TRANS.)

# Bahnhofskonzert

Kein Atmen mehr. Das Firmament – voll Maden.
Verstummt die Sterne, keiner glüht.
Doch über uns, Gott siehts, Musik, dort oben –
Der Bahnhof bebt vom Aonidenlied.
Und wieder ist die Luft, zerrissen von Signalen,
die Geigenluft die ineinanderfließt.

Der Riesenpark. Die Bahnhofskugel, gläsern.
Die Eisenwelt – verzaubert, abermals.
Und feierlich, in Richtung Nebel-Eden,
Zu einem Klang-Gelage rollt die Bahn.
Ein Pfauenschrei. Klaviergetöse.
Ich kam zu spät. Ich träum ja. Mir ist bang.

Der Glaswald rings, ich habe ihn betreten.
Der Geigen-Bau – in Tränen, aufgewühlt.
Der Duft der Rosen in den Moder-Beeten;
der Chor der Nacht, der anhebt, wild.
Der teure einst, der mitzog, er, der Schatten . . .
Sein Nachtquartier: ein gläsernes Gezelt . . .

Die Eisenwelt, sie schäumt, schäumt vor Musik –
Mir ist, als bebte sie am ganzen Leibe –
Ich steh im Glasflur, lehne mich zurück.
Wo willst du hin? Es ist die Totenfeier
des Schattens, der dort ging. Noch einmal war Musik.

1921

Holly Cundiff (trans.)

# Railway Station Concert

Breathing no more. The firmament – full of maggots.
The stars speechless, not one burning,
Yet God above us sees music overhead there –
The railway trembling to the Song of Ages.
And the breeze is anew, blasted by signals,
The violin air wafting in and out.

The depot sphere crystal clear.
The enchanted iron-world, anew.
And enchanted, toward foggy-Eden:
One clanging cacophony arriving at the railroad.
A peacock crying. Piano din.
I come too late. Anxiously, I must be dreaming.

The surrounding woods of glass: I have trod them.
The violin sequence – builds – with stirring tears.
The scent of the roses in the musty garden-beds:
The choir of the night increasingly savage.
The dear one once, who marched along, he, the shadow . . .
His night lodgings: a glassy canopy.

The iron-world, one overflowing, foam before music –
Was to me as it trembled with bodies undivided –
I stand in the hall, resting my back.
Where do you want to go? It is the burial rite
Of the shadow that passed there. Once again there was music.

1921

11. Henri Michaux

# Icebergs

Icebergs, sans garde-fou, sans ceinture, où de vieux cormorans abattus et les âmes des matelots morts récemment viennent s'accouder aux nuits enchanteresses de l'hyperboréal.

Icebergs, Icebergs, cathédrales sans religion de l'hiver éternel, enrobés dans la calotte glaciaire de la planète Terre.

Combien hauts, combien purs sont tes bords enfantés par le froid.

Icebergs, Icebergs, dos du Nord-Atlantique, augustes Bouddhas gelés sur des mers incontemplées. Phares scintillants de la Mort sans issue, le cri éperdu du silence dure des siècles.

Icebergs, Icebergs, Solitaires sans besoin, des pays bouchés, distants, et libres de vermine. Parents des îles, parents des sources, comme je vous vois, comme vous m'êtes familiers . . .

1934

Paul Celan (trans.)

# Eisberge

Eisberge, gurtlos, geländerlos, wo alte abgekämpfte Kormorane und die Seelen der kürzlich verstorbenen Matrosen an den hyperboräischen Zaubernächte Stütze finden und Halt.

Eisberge, Eisberge, religionslose Dome des ewigen Winters, von der Eiskappe des Planeten Erde umkleidet.
Wie sind sie hoch, wie sind sie rein, deine frostgeborenen Ränder.

Eisberge, Eisberge, Rücken des Nord-Atlantiks, erhabne, auf ungeschauten Meeren zu Eis erstarrte Buddhas, Blinkfeuer des ausweglosen Todes, der desperate Schrei der Stille halt Jahrhunderte an.

Eisberge, Eisberge, grundlos Einsame der zugemauerten Länder,
Abstand wahrend und frei von Geschmeiß. Eltern der Inseln,
Eltern der Quellen, wie gut ich euch sehe, wie vertraut ihr mir seid . . .

1934

Holly Cundiff (trans.)

# Icebergs

Icebergs, ungirded without terrain, where displaced old cormorants and souls of newly deceased sailors find a foothold in magic nights.

Icebergs, icebergs, irreligious dome of the eternal winters from the icecaps veiling the planet Earth.
How high they are, how pure they are, your borders born from frost.

Icebergs, icebergs, backbones of the North Atlantic, exalted, on seas unseen, icy Buddhas stiffen toward the flashing lights of hopeless death, a desperate cry holds a century of silence.

Icebergs, icebergs, the unfathomed Solitary of barricaded lands, elders of the isles, elders of the spring, O I see you so well, O how familiar you are to me . . .

1934

12. Antonin Artaud

# Prière

Ah donne-nous des crânes de braises
Des crânes brûlés aux foudres du ciel
Des crânes lucides des crânes réels
Et traversés de ta présence

Fais-nous naître aux cieux du dedans
Criblés de gouffres en averses
Et qu'un vertige nous traverse
Avec un ongle incandescent

Rassasie-nous nous avons faim
De commotions inter-sidérales
Ah verse-nous des laves astrales
A la place de notre sang

Détache-nous. Divise-nous
Avec tes mains de braises coupantes
Ouvre-nous ces voûtes brûlantes
Où l'on meurt plus loin que la mort

Fais vaciller notre cerveau
Au sein de sa propre science
Et ravis-nous l'intelligence
Aux griffes d'un typhon nouveau.

Paul Celan (trans.)

# Gebet

Glutschädel gib uns, Schädel
versengt von Himmelsstrahl,
klaräugig, wirklich und wahr,
durchwest von dir.

Laß uns die Leibesfrucht sein
der Innenhimmel,
reiß Abgrund um Abgrund durch uns,
fahr mit dem Nagel drein,
laß ihn Wirbel und Weißglut sein.

Wir hungern
nach schütterndem Sternraum:
still unsern Hunger.
Gieß uns die Blutbahn voll
mit Sternenlaven.

Mach uns los.
Zerteil uns
mit schneidender Gluthand.
Schließ uns auf
das Brandgewölbe, darin
man über den Tod hinausstirbt.

Laß unser Hirn erbeben
tief im Gewußten.
Raub uns unsre Vernunft
mit den Fängen der neuen
Taifune.

Holly Cundiff (trans.)

# Prayer

Glowing-skull give us, skull,
scorched from rays of heaven
clear-eyed, genuine and true,
imbued with you.

Let us be the embryo
of the inner heavens,
rend chasm after chasm through us.
Drive the nail in there,
white-heat, let it whirl.

Hunger after
trembling stars:
our quiet longing.
Pour our bloodstream full
of star lava.

Let us free.
Divide us
with keen burning-hands.
Open us into
the suffocating canopy of fire, in this
we die beyond death.

Let our minds raise.
Deeply know.
Rob us our reason
Enthralled with the catches
Typhoons.

13. Charles Baudelaire

# La mort des pauvres

C'est la Mort qui console, hélas! et qui fait vivre;
C'est le but de la vie, et c'est le seul espoir
Qui, comme un élixir, nous monte et nous enivre,
Et nous donne le cœur de marcher jusqu'au soir;

À travers la tempête, et la neige, et le givre,
C'est la clarté vibrante à notre horizon noir;
C'est l'auberge fameuse inscrite sur le livre,
Où l'on pourra manger, et dormir, et s'asseoir;

C'est un Ange qui tient dans ses doigts magnétiques
Le sommeil et le don des rêves extatiques,
Et qui refait le lit des gens pauvres et nus;

C'est la gloire des dieux, c'est le grenier mystique,
C'est la bourse du pauvre et sa patrie antique,
C'est le portique ouvert sur les Cieux inconnus!

Paul Celan (trans.)

# Der Tod der Armen

Der Tod ists, ach, der tröstet, er flößt dir Leben ein;
wohin du lebst, da ist er, er ist die Zuversicht,
die zaubrisch in dir hochsteigt, berauschend wie ein Wein:
das Herz trinkt sich hier Mut zu – eh's Nacht wird, stockt es nicht.

Wenn dich die Wetter peitschen, Reif fällt und Flocke weht,
ist er der Schwärze Lichtsaum, auf ihn hältst du dann zu,
ist er der Krug, die Gaststatt, von der geschrieben steht,
hier seien Tisch und Speise, das Lager und die Ruh.

Er ist der Schlummerengel, sein Finger zieht und bannt,
das Träumen und Entrücktsein, er schenkts und teilt er aus,
und wer da arm und bloß ist, den bettet seine Hand.

Er ist der Götter Glorie, das speichernde, das Haus,
der Armen Zehrung ist er und ist ihr Heimatland,
er baut die Säulengänge zu Himmeln ungekannt.

Holly Cundiff (trans.)

# The Death of the Poor

It is death, alas, that comforts, imbuing you with life;
wherever you live, there he is, it is the confidence
that magically lifts you up in the heady wine:
here the heart drinks to its courage before night comes, it doesn't stop beating.

When the weather whips you, frost and snowflakes blow,
he is the light's edge of the blackness – on him you cling tight,
it is the tavern, the mug of sweet stuff, of which it is written,
here were said to be the table and meal, lodging and rest.

It is the slumber-angel, his finger charms and beckons,
dreaming and enraptured he bestows and disperses it,
his hand blessing the bed for whomever is there poor and naked.

Death is the glory of the gods, the house of cumulation,
he is the provider of the poor, their homeland,
he builds colonnaded paths to heavens unknown.

14. Emily Dickinson

# My life closed twice before its close

My life closed twice before its close;
It yet remains to see
If Immortality unveil
A third event to me,

So huge, so hopeless to conceive,
As these that twice befell.
Parting is all we know of heaven,
And all we need of hell.

Paul Celan (trans.)

# Mein Leben, zweimal fiels ins Schloß

Mein Leben, zweimal fiels ins Schloß,
    eh's zufällt; nun, ich will
jetzt sehn, ob die Unsterblichkeit
    ein Drittes mir enthüllt,

so ohne Hoffnung und so groß.
    Abschied, das ist, was uns,
du Himmel, an dir wißbar ist, –
    und Hölle ists genug.

Holly Cundiff (trans.)

# My life shut twice before it closed

My life shut twice
    before it closed, now on I want
to see, if in this immortality
    a third life revealed to me,

so without hope and so long,
    this farewell, Heaven is all
of you that can be known, –
    and of hell, it is enough.

15. Emily Dickinson

# To my quick ear the Leaves – conferred

To my quick ear the Leaves – conferred –
The Bushes – they were Bells –
I could not find a Privacy
From Nature's setinels –

In Cave if I presumed to hide
The Walls – begun to tell –
Creation seemed a mighty Crack –
To make me visible –

Paul Celan (trans.)

# Die Blätter traten vor mein Ohr

Die Blätter traten vor mein Ohr,
    der Busch war Glockenschall.
Kein Bei-mir-selbst-Sein – die Natur
    hat Augen überall.

Wollt ich hinunter ins Gewölb,
    schon sprachs da auf mich ein.
Ein Klaffen, das mich sichtbar macht:
    *das* muß die Schöpfung sein.

Holly Cundiff (trans.)

# The leaves were drifting by my ear

The leaves were drifting by my ear,
    The bush was bells clanging.
Not being-by-myself – this is nature
    possessing eyes everywhere.

If I wanted to enter the chamber,
    speak to me here.
A yawning that makes me visible:
    *that* must be the Creation.

16. André du Bouchet

# Embrasure

Notre visage, comme un mur, heurté par le même feu.
Comme le froid dans l'horizon compact.

J'effleure, sur la terre serrée, ce front qui se hisse à côté
de moi.

L'autre distance qui fait écho au front, à travers cette
trop grande chaleur, comme le corps infime de l'été.

Tout fuit à travers l'eau immobile, les souffles de l'air.

La route liée nous est rendue en feu.

Je ne me suis habitué au jour
qu'à la fin du jour.

Le feu brûle aujourd'hui sous un autre nom.

Paul Celan (trans.)

# Türöffnung

Unser Gesicht, wie eine Mauer, angestoßen von demselben Feuer.
Wie die Kälte am kompakten Horizont.

Leise berühre ich, auf gedrungener Erde, diese Stirn, die sich emporhißt an meiner Seite.

Die andre Entfernung, die der Stirn nachklingt, quer durch diese allzu große Glut, wie der winzige Leib des Sommers.

Alles flüchtet durch das reglose Wasser, durch allen Lufthauch.

Die gebundene Straße wird uns zurückgegeben in Flammen.

Erst am Ende des Tags habe ich mich
gewöhnt an den Tag.

Das Feuer brennt heute unter einem andern Namen.

Holly Cundiff (trans.)

# Doorway

Our face, like a wall, buttressed against the same fire
Like this coldness on the solid horizon.

On compacted earth I softly touch this brow that raises itself on my side.

The other distance, that echoes the brow sloping through this virulent heat,
like the slender body of summer.

Everything flees the motionless water through every breath of air.

The blocked street will be returned to us in flames.

Only at day's end have I gotten
used to the day.

The fire burns today under another name.

17. Osip Mandelstam

# Silentium

Она еще не родилась,
Она и музыка и слово,
И потому всего живого
Ненарушаемая связь.

Спокойно дышат моря груди,
Но, как безумный, светел день,
И пены бледная сирень
В мутно-лазоревом сосуде.

Да обретут мои уста
Первоначальную немоту,
Как кристаллическую ноту,
Что от рождения чиста!

Останься пеной, Афродита,
И слово в музыку вернись,
И сердце сердца устыдись,
С первоосновой жизни слито!

1910

Paul Celan (trans.)

# Silentium

Sie ist noch nicht, ist unentstanden,
Musik ist sie und Wort:
so lebt, verknüpft durch ihre Bande,
was west und atmet, fort.

Im Meer das Atmen, ruhig, immer,
das Licht durchwächst den Raum;
aus dem Gefäß, das bläulich schimmert,
steigt fliederblasser Schaum.

O könnt ich doch, mit meinem Munde,
solch erstes Schweigen sein,
ein Ton, kristallen, aus dem Grunde,
und so geboren: rein.

Bleib, Aphrodite, dieses Schäumen,
du Wort, geh, bleib Musik.
Des Herzens schäm dich, Herz, das seinem
Beginn und Grund entstieg.

1910

Holly Cundiff (trans.)

# Silentium

She is not yet, uncreated,
she is music and words:
thus bound by her ribbon,
whatever exists and breathes endures.

In the sea the breathing, always tranquil,
the light spreads through the room;
radiating bluish from the bowl
lilac-pale spume rises.

If only I could be such,
a first silence, with my mouth,
a sound, crystalline, from the earth,
and so born: pure.

Stay this effervescence, Aphrodite,
you word, go, remain music.
The foundation arisen, beginning,
Heart, be shy of the heart.

1910

18. Giuseppe Ungaretti

# Finale

Piú non muggisce, non sussurra il mare,
Il mare.

Senza i sogni, incolore campo è il mare,
Il mare.

Fa pietà anche il mare,
Il mare.

Muovono nuvole irriflesse il mare,
Il mare.

A fumi tristi cedé il letto il mare,
Il mare.

Morto è anche, vedi, il mare,
Il mare.

Paul Celan (trans.)

# Finale

Nicht mehr brüllt es, nicht mehr flüsterts, das Meer,
das Meer.

Ohne die Träume ist es ein fahles Feld, das Meer,
das Meer.

Erbarmen tuts einem, auch das, das Meer,
das Meer.

Ungespiegelte Wolken bewegens, das Meer,
das Meer.

Tristem Rauch tritt es sein Bett ab, das Meer,
das Meer.

Auch tot ist, du siehsts, das Meer,
das Meer.

Holly Cundiff (trans.)

# Finale

It bellows no more, whispers no more, the Sea,
the Sea.

It is a field, fallow without a dream, the Sea,
the Sea.

It does pity one, that too, the Sea,
the Sea.

It stirs unreflected clouds, the Sea,
the Sea.

Cheerless smoke surrenders its bed, the Sea,
the Sea.

You see it's dead also, the Sea,
the Sea.

Published by Marquand Books, Seattle © 2024
www.marquandbooks.com



Edited by Scott Thompson and Michelle Piranio
Designed by Thomas Eykemans
Proofread by Bruno George
Typeset in Warnock and Futura PT
Printed in China by Artron Art Group on 120gsm Milan Neutral paper

Available through:
ARTBOOK | D.A.P.
75 Broad Street, Suite 630
New York, NY 10004
www.artbook.com

Library of Congress Control Number: 2024939130
ISBN 978-1-64657-043-0